Contents

Why Do You Write Poetry?

Many people want to be creative in some way. Some people sketch or paint, others dance or sing or play an instrument. Brian Moses writes words on paper.

I started to write poetry when I realized that I couldn't write songs.

Initially, I played around with a guitar and tried to write like my hero Bob Dylan, but I wasn't very good on the guitar. Because I wanted to write, poetry seemed the next best way to express myself.

Now I write because I'm fortunate enough to see my poems published in books and to be paid for them. But I also write because I need to.

I couldn't ever think of giving up writing. It's a part of me, it is what I do, and it gives me immense enjoyment and satisfaction.

When I first started writing, my father said to me, 'Brian, writing poems is OK but it'll never earn you a living.' Sadly he wasn't alive to see that he was wrong, and that poetry has earned me a very good living for the past twenty years.

I remember the first poem I wrote. It was for a girl who lived up the road from me. I wanted to go out with her so I wrote her a poem. I spent ages getting it right. Then one night I plucked up courage and popped the poem through her letterbox. Unfortunately she went out with someone else. I think I'm over her now though!
Brian Moses

Brian Moses is one of Britain's most popular children's poets who loves performing to all sorts of audiences.

What the Poets Say

'Poets write because they have to. It's something inside driving you on. Writers and other creative people often ask themselves, "Why am I doing this?" But they very rarely consider stopping, even though the writing process can be difficult, frustrating and even painful. And there's one reason a poet will never give for writing poetry: to get rich!'
Roger Stevens

'I think poetry writing is probably a disease – but I don't want to be cured!'
Clare Bevan

'I never set out to be a poet. By a process of experimentation I discovered it's what I write best, I think. And above all, I just love words. I'm not interested in stories or characters or plots. I simply want to play with language, with words. And I do.'
James Carter

'I write poetry because I'm fascinated by words. I like playing with words, their sounds and their meanings. I like trying to write different forms of poetry, too.'
John Foster

'For me, writing poetry is a joy. It's very rewarding and satisfying to have written something that might make other people laugh, or cry. I like it best when they laugh but if they cry, it means that they recognize something sad that we can both share.'
John Rice

'Why do I write? Because I want to change the world. I'm not a politician or anything, so I realize that maybe I can just change people's minds, and get them to think and look at things differently.'
Benjamin Zephaniah

Where Do You Get Your Ideas From?

This is the most common question that poets are asked when they visit schools.

My reply is that poets are idea detectives, always on the hunt for different ideas that may inspire poems. I find my ideas in the places that I visit. I wrote a poem about a mummified foot that I found in a museum in Cheltenham, and another about the discovery that you can actually get married at London Zoo. Adrian Mitchell's ideas come from conversations heard on buses and trains. Valerie Bloom says that she tries to be acutely aware of everything around her.

All poets will tell you that they have many more ideas for poems than they ever get round to completing. Brian Patten writes, 'All I know is that as soon as you get one, another comes along, then another, then another. . . And then they go away for a while, and I think that I'll never be able to write another poem again.'

It is really important to write down ideas the moment they come along.

An idea is a bit like a knock on the door. Ignore the knocking and whoever it is goes away. So, too, will the idea. Ignore it and you won't remember it later. It will disappear. As a poet, I can't afford to lose ideas, so I grab them the moment I think of them. I may be driving the car, or taking a bath, or doing the weekly shop, but the most important thing is to stop what I'm doing and write down the idea on a scrap of paper or in my notebook.

Top ten sources for ideas

1 Places
2 Watching people
3 Conversations
4 Memories
5 Families
6 Newspapers
7 Television
8 Animals
9 Daydreams
10 Childhood

Unusual events like this wedding at London Zoo can provide some great ideas.

What the Poets Say

'I was sitting in a school staffroom on one occasion when I listened to six teachers all telling each other what they wore in bed! I sat and made notes then wrote a poem called, "What Teachers Wear in Bed". This led to a book called *The Secret Lives of Teachers* which is often bought by teachers as well as children!'
Brian Moses

'Once I was sitting on a beach in Devon when three real elephants wandered past me and paddled in the waves! Two years later I wrote a poem called "Elephants on the Beach".'
Clare Bevan

'I love travelling and talking to people in various parts of the world; when I listen to their joys and fears I get most inspired.'
Benjamin Zephaniah

This poet is writing down ideas in his notebook at a club.

'One thing you can never be short of is ideas. They are around us all the time. From the moment you wake until you go to bed there are ideas everywhere. Even in bed – in your dreams – there are ideas.'
Roger Stevens

'The old literature of Ireland . . . has been the chief illumination of my imagination all my life.'
W B Yeats, 1865-1939

'Anything can spark a poem, from the smallest thing to the largest. I like things like pebbles and twigs, ordinary humble things that you might take for granted. I like to squeeze meanings out of them.'
Tony Mitton

'I think most writers write out of a mixture of remembering, observing and imagining. What happens to me is quite often I start with a memory, mix it with observations of people I know and then mix in a bit of "What if. . .?" '
Michael Rosen

Where Do You Like to Write?

I often find that I don't always have a choice of where I want to write. An idea comes along and it needs attention. So I pick up a piece of paper and work on the poem wherever I happen to be.

Fortunately, in my house, I'm never far away from a notebook or a pile of old envelopes, and many poems have started life at the kitchen table over an early morning cup of tea.

Most poets will tell you that poems often demand to be written at the most awkward moments. I often have ideas for poems when I'm rushing to get out of the house first thing in the morning. Then I'm dashing from the washbasin to the scrap of paper, scribbling lines down so quickly and so messily that I'll have trouble understanding them later on.

I wrote one poem – 'Snake Hotel' – on an intercity train travelling from London to Edinburgh. I got the idea from the late Steve Irwin, the Crocodile Hunter, when he talked about the snake hotel at the back of his house. I wrote that down in my notebook and happened to glance at it while on the train. I pictured a five star hotel staffed by snakes, and by the time I reached Edinburgh I'd written the poem.

Beaches are good places too, as I get bored sitting in the sun and need to occupy myself in some way. But my main writing place is an office in my garden that was formerly a double garage. Out went the cars and in came the computers, writing desks and thousands of books!

Top ten places where poets like to write

1. On trains
2. In cafes
3. In bed
4. In studies
5. In sheds
6. On beaches
7. In hotels
8. In the garden
9. On planes
10. In the kitchen

Some poets like to write on a laptop outside in a park.

What the Poets Say

'My office is a large room with a huge desk, a pinball machine, a bar stocked with chocolate and milkshake, a massive music system, a TV screen that takes up a whole wall and a giant electric train set. It's on the top of a mountain in Spain overlooking the sea. Well . . . I'm stretching the truth a little here. Actually it's in the corner of the only living room in a small flat in the middle of London.'
Roger Stevens

'The strangest places I've written a poem are on top of a snow-covered mountain in Italy, and in the bath. I had to get out of the bath quickly and get the words down on paper before they disappeared!'
John Foster

This is the room where Michael Rosen writes.

'I write in a stone building (called The Hut) in the grounds of my vast garden on the North York Moors. Nearby is a rushing moorland stream known as Thorgill Beck. Usually my cat Rusty sleeps in a box under the table while I write at the computer.'
Wes Magee

'I write in cafes, where nobody knows me. I like to sit there with a coffee or two, a cake or three, a notebook, my thesaurus and my rhyming dictionary.'
Mike Jubb

'My office is in the attic of a converted chapel. As I look out I can see the village rooftops, the local church and behind that, the green hills of Shropshire.'
Andrew Fusek Peters

'These days I have the use of a little starter home in the daytime. I call it The Hutch as there are no windows or doors at the back. So I go rabbiting on in my hutch, you could say. I prefer to be alone and in silence.'
Tony Mitton

What Do You Need to Write Your Poems?

Some writers of fiction say that they can only write in one particular place, perhaps sitting at their desk with everything arranged neatly around them.

This is probably because fiction writers need to have their whole story, or at least what has been written so far, on the computer screen or inside a hardback notebook, so that they can refer to what is already there while trying to write more.

Poets are much more adaptable. They seem to be able to write anywhere.

Wherever I go I take my Dictaphone. I find, quite often, that some poems arrive in a rush of ideas that tumble out of my head too quickly for me to write down. A Dictaphone solves that problem. I have 'written' many poems on my Dictaphone, capturing ideas that would otherwise have been difficult to note down.

Often ideas come when I'm driving, so I can pull over to the side of the road and quickly record lines of a possible poem. With a machine that is voice-activated I can even leave it switched on so that it starts to record when I start to speak.

Dictaphones like this are easy to use and great for recording ideas.

I remember one occasion when I was driving from Guildford towards London along the A3. I had what I thought was a great idea for a poem and spent half an hour or so recording my ideas. When I reached my destination I went to play back the tape and found nothing. The batteries had been flat! I wrote the poem again but I'm sure it wasn't as good.

Brian Moses

What the Poets Say

'Usually 2B pencils . . . or fun pencils, with parrots or spots on – that kind of thing! Later, when the poem is nearly ready, I try it on the computer . . . but usually end up scribbling all over it again several times before the final version.'
Judith Nicholls

A good strong notebook like this is ideal for writing your notes and poems.

'I have to write in notebooks first – I have loads of them. Can't write poems straight onto the computer.'
Paul Cookson

'Time (as much as I can grab). Silence (although I'm quite good at switching my ears off). Paper (any size will do). Pencils or pens (my favourite is a fat, black fountain pen). And a cat or two for company.'
Clare Bevan

'I need ye olde pen and ye olde envelope! Writing poems on a computer is a very bad idea. Honestly. Roger McGough says that it looks too good too quickly on the screen . . . And why an envelope? Because Paul McCartney wrote the lyrics to 'Hey Jude' on the back of an old envelope. If it's good enough for him. . .'
James Carter

'If you asked me what equipment I think a writer needs, my first answer would not be a computer. I think it is more important for a writer to have a good eye and a sharp ear.'
Karla Kuskin

How Do You Find the Rhymes?

Rhyme and rhythm are all around us: in the nursery rhymes we hear as children, in playground chants and games, in the advertising jingles that get stuck in our heads and in the songs we listen to.

The American poet Lillian Morrison explains how we live in a rhythmical universe, '. . . from the dance of atoms and our own heartbeats to the ocean tides and movement of the planets.' She says that when she writes, she sometimes feels in touch with that universal rhythm.

Yet rhymes don't always come easily, even for the professional poet.

I'm always trying to discard the ordinary rhymes and look for pairs of words that say something fresh. It's an ambition I don't always fulfil!

I challenge myself first of all to see if I can summon up rhymes that will sound natural to the flow of the piece and fit its meaning. So often a poorly chosen rhyme can spoil a poem. If I'm really stuck then I'll reach for the rhyming dictionary.

I do love Allan Ahlberg's rhymes and am particularly impressed with a couplet from a long poem of his called 'The Mighty Slide'. Ice has covered the school playground and there is a queue of children waiting to try out a slide, although Denis is hesitant:

His wobbly style is unmistakable:
The sign of a boy who knows he's breakable.

Of course, poems don't have to rhyme, but they do need a rhythm. In poetry that doesn't rhyme (free verse), this may come from repetition of a line or words, or it may be helped by words that sound good or 'chime' when they are placed near to each other.

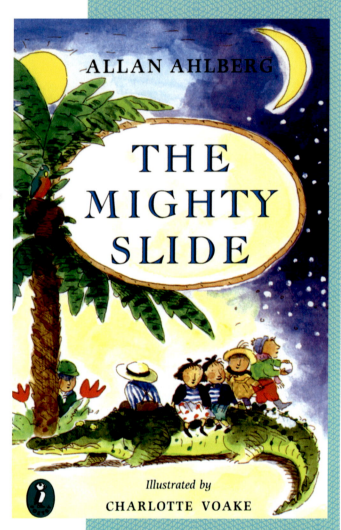

ALLAN AHLBERG

THE MIGHTY SLIDE

Illustrated by
CHARLOTTE VOAKE

Allan Ahlberg's book *The Mighty Slide* has some great rhymes.

12

What the Poets Say

'The thesaurus and the rhyming dictionary work hand in hand for me. If, for instance, I write a line that ends in "shout" and I can't find a rhyme that has the rhythm and meaning that I need for the next line, then I throw "shout" away and look for an alternative like "yell" or "holler". Then I start all over again, looking for a suitable rhyme. Writing rhyming poetry involves a lot of problem solving.'
Mike Jubb

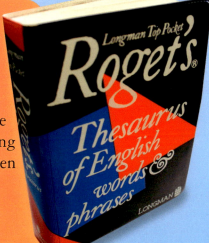

A thesaurus is a very useful book for a poet because it lists words with similar meanings.

'When my brain is in exactly the right gear for poetry, the rhymes seem to happen automatically. When the cogs and wheels start to stick and rattle, I fool around with sounds and make a horrible mess in the margins. When everything goes CLUNK . . . I have a trusty old dictionary to jump-start my ideas again.'
Clare Bevan

'I used to live near Lewes in Sussex. When I was looking for a house I noticed there was an estate agent called Roland Gorringe. Immediately I wrote a poem about it. Why? So I could use the rhyme. Can you guess it. . .?'
Roger Stevens

'I like to twist words round and find unusual ways of rhyming or stretching words into rhymes – the cornier the better!'
Paul Cookson

'I especially like to play around with echoes/near rhymes inside the lines, to add to the music: home/dream, mind/sand, gone/alone. . .'
Judith Nicholls

'My favourite rhyme that I've come up with is from a poem called "Electric Guitars":
". . .bass, lead and rhythm,/I basically dig 'em".'
James Carter

How Do You Cope With Writers' Block?

I don't think that poets suffer from this quite as much as fiction writers. I know that I sometimes have a few weeks when I don't write very much and then suddenly several ideas come along. This used to worry me but it doesn't any more as I am now confident that when time and circumstances are right, ideas will flow again.

The worst thing to do is to panic and get stressed about writers' block. It's far better to leave whatever it is that's causing the problem behind for a while, and get on with something else. If I do hit a problem with something that needs doing straightaway, I'll go outside and take the dog for a walk or clean out the chicken house. I then find that on my return I can get going again on my writing.

Occasionally temporary writers' block is a problem at the start of a day's work. I sit down with paper in front of me or stare at the blank screen, knowing that I need to write but I can't think where to begin.

One way I try to overcome this is by doing a five minute 'splurge'. For five minutes I just write down anything that comes into my head. It seems to have the effect of freeing up ideas and setting them in motion again.

Some poets find that going for a walk helps them overcome writers' block.

'I don't often suffer from writers' block because I always have several projects on at once and if I get stuck on one I switch to another. That's the good thing about writing in different genres.'
Valerie Bloom

'If poetry comes not as naturally as the leaves to a tree it had better not come at all.'
John Keats, 1795-1823

'For me writing comes in bursts of activity with long stretches of nothing in between. When I'm not writing I forget how much I like it when I am.'
Brian Patten

'Unless something interests you or excites you or belongs to your life in a deep way, then you just cannot think of anything to say about it. The words will not come.'
Ted Hughes, 1930-1998

'I think writers' block is a myth myself. If I believed in it I might be tempted to catch it, which I can't afford. But I think if you're a writer you just write. There's never a shortage of subject matter.'
Tony Mitton

Benjamin Zephaniah is one of Britain's most popular poets.

'I believe that spending time not writing is as important as writing. So I like to come away from being creative for a while, then I can come back to it with a fresh mind.'
Benjamin Zephaniah

How Do You Know When a Poem is Finished?

I'm always telling children how the last line or two of a poem should 'do something' for the reader. It might make them smile or laugh, it might make them feel a bit sad or shivery, or it might make them wonder.

Inevitably, it's often the hardest part of a poem to write. It can't be just another line that could slot into the poem anywhere. It must give that sense of completeness.

If I'm lucky enough to have the beginning of a poem and I've also thought how it should end, then I rarely have too much trouble linking the two. But I have many poems hanging around in my notebooks that remain uncompleted, many poems that I should like to finish but just can't.

When you have been writing for a long time, you develop that 'gut feeling' for an ending. It never fails to excite too, as you rush to write down lines that you know will be right.

Valerie Bloom engrossed in performing one of her poems at the Children's Poetry Bookshelf Competition prize-giving celebration.

Longest time to write a poem

The longest time it took me to complete a poem was nine years. I was in Canada and I saw a dog hit by a car. I went into a cafe and wrote down a few lines, wrote a few more back at my hotel and more on the flight home. But that important final line or two just wouldn't come. I must have taken the poem out every year for nine years until suddenly, when I read it through, I knew what I had to write to finish it.

The shortest time it took me to write a poem was about ninety seconds. It was a haiku written after looking out at the lawn one morning. It went like this:

*Droppings on the lawn
left by night-shopping hedgehogs
leaving Slugs 'R' Us*

Brian Moses

What the Poets Say

'A poem is *never* finished! I'm a perfectionist and there's always a little extra tweak or change you can make to improve or develop a poem. What I look for in my poems is: a) originality – something fresh, a new way of looking at something; b) tightness – the poem has really got to flow; and c) every single word has to earn its place – if it doesn't, it has to go.'
James Carter

Reading or performing a poem aloud to an audience, as Polly Dunbar is doing here with one of her books, can change the way a poet finishes the poem.

'The more you write, the better you get at deciding if something's finished. But if your work is edited for publication then you sometimes have to consider the opinions of others – if you want to get it published.'
Tony Mitton

'Sometimes I'm tempted to rewrite poems that I wrote years ago. This is not usually a good idea. When I've done this I've often made the poem a bit different, which is quite interesting, I suppose, but rarely have I made it any better. Once you're happy with a poem I think it's best to leave it alone.'
Roger Stevens

'The more you write, the more you get a "feel" for when a poem is as good as you can get it.'
Mike Jubb

'Often a poem seems finished on the page but then takes on a different life in performance. I think poems only really come alive when being performed – you need to find the right voice, rhythm, speed, tone, timing etc. Poems often change with repeated performances as you grow into them.'
Paul Cookson

Does Anyone Help You With Your Poetry?

I always show my poems to my wife or my daughters. They know that I want genuine criticism even if I don't always agree with what they say at the time. Later on, when I look at the poem again, I find that they are usually right. I'm too close to the poem, too protective of it, but they are able to stand back and see what's wrong.

Sometimes another writer will take a look at something I've written. My good friend, the poet Pie Corbett, and I, have a long history of showing each other things that we've written. We trust each other's judgement and know that any criticism will be positive, with suggestions as to how a word or a line might be replaced.

In the past I have written poems with Pie, in particular on a trip to New York that we took together. We were walking down Madison Avenue when we saw a sign that said, 'Lost Cat: $500 reward.' Both of us reached for our notebooks and we sat in a cafe scribbling down ideas. After a while we pooled our ideas and changed the title 'Lost Cat in New York' to 'Lost Kitty in New York City.' We very soon had the poem written, although we made a few small changes when we looked at it again on the flight home. We also wrote another poem called 'New York Attitude' which we performed together at the Cheltenham Book Festival a month later.

Editors, too, often comment on poems that poets want to put into their books. My editor at publisher Macmillan, Gaby Morgan, with whom I have worked for many years now, is someone whose opinion I trust.

Poetry workshops and groups, like this one run by Welsh poet and author Catrin Dafydd, provide opportunities to show poems and get help with them.

'I read them to my wife and children, fully expecting them to fall down and worship me as the next laureate-in-the-making. Do they do that? No!! Instead, my wife will unhelpfully make suggestions for redrafting and dare to criticize my carefully crafted lines. (Well, all right, we all need a little help sometimes, I admit it!)'
Andrew Fusek Peters

'Show what you write to people you respect. Listen to what they say.'
Michael Rosen

'When I finish a poem I like to torture my family by forcing them to listen to it.'
Clare Bevan

'I always feel pleased when I've written a new poem, so I print it out and show it to my wife Chris. Then I wait anxiously to see how she reacts. . . She always spots the words that I've been struggling to get right and there are quite a few poems in which I've made changes as a result of what she said.'
John Foster

'I always read newly finished poems to Rusty (my cat). Sometimes I sit beside my garden pond and try them out on the goldfish and ghost carp, but they quickly get bored and swim away.'
Wes Magee

What's the Best Thing About Being a Poet?

I keep thinking that I have discovered the answer to this question, but fortunately, every now and then, something else happens and then that becomes 'my best thing' for a while.

Like many of the poets questioned, I would probably say that the ten reasons given to the right just about sum up why I love doing what I do. I've been very fortunate to have worked as a full-time writer for the past twenty years. I have had many books published and been invited to perform my poems in locations as different as Iceland, the Edinburgh Festival, Prince Charles's Summer School for teachers, an open prison, a New York bookshop and RAF schools on Cyprus.

I never quite know what's going to happen next - an email will arrive inviting me to travel somewhere, or there'll be a telephone call from a publisher with good news, or a school will ring and tell me how they've been reading my poems and could I visit. It is this unpredictability that keeps the job exciting and rewarding.

Ten answers to this question that were given to me by poets I interviewed:

1 Being your own boss
2 Not having to get up early every morning for work
3 Being allowed to daydream
4 Having a creative job
5 Making people laugh
6 Being paid to show off when performing poems
7 Travelling all over the UK and abroad
8 Encouraging children to develop their writing
9 Having a book published
10 Having fun when I'm playing with words

Michael Rosen, Valerie Bloom and Wes Magee were invited to judge the Children's Poetry Bookshelf competition in 2007.

What the Poets Say

'The very best thing is thinking, "I'm pleased with this poem." But there are other brilliant rewards. . . I love it when a poem appears in a proper printed anthology. I love it when an artist gives my poem a fantastically fabulous illustration. And I love it when I read a poem out loud, and the audience laughs, or sighs, or gasps, or cries in just the right place.'
Clare Bevan

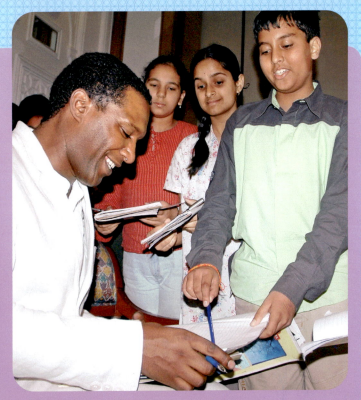

British poet Lemn Sissay signs autographs in Hyderabad in India.

'It's an interesting and peculiar life. I see it as a kind of patchwork, made up of quite distinct and different squares, contiguous but not overlapping. When I go to bed at night, quite often I have no idea what I'm doing the following day until I look at my diary. It could be anything from working on a radio script, writing a children's book, doing my one-man show in a school, teaching at university, writing a prose poem or just playing about with one or some of my children.'
Michael Rosen

'My proudest moment as a poet was when I saw my first book of solo poems, *I Did Not Eat the Goldfish,* for the first time. It had a great cover and I was really pleased with the poems that I'd written. At that moment I thought, "I've made it. I really am a proper children's poet".'
Roger Stevens

'Proudest moments: writing a poem about Brian Labone (ex-Everton Football Club captain from the '60s and early '70s) and seeing it used in the match-day programme and also read at his funeral by Ian Callaghan (ex-Liverpool and England player); Noddy Holder (lead singer of the rock group Slade) writing an introduction for my book and saying that I was "Slade's Poet Laureate".'
Paul Cookson

Do You Enjoy Performing Your Poetry?

I began performing my poetry whilst at teacher training college where I also met up with Pie Corbett. He and I then became part of a six-man group of poets and musicians performing poetry and rock 'n' roll in clubs, pubs, schools and at festivals. This is where I learnt my stagecraft and also the techniques that I use in my poetry and percussion shows today.

Andrew Fusek Peters is a very lively performer of his poems.

Like most of the poets I know, I love to perform my poems to an appreciative audience, and fortunately I am able to do so regularly in schools and libraries. I have a show that lasts an hour and have learned to pace it carefully, starting with something loud, then quietening down, then lifting it again and so on towards a big finish! I like to include poems that I hope will make children (and teachers) smile and laugh, others that will make them think, and one or two that might make them shiver. I use percussion instruments to underpin the rhythms of many of the poems and in a couple of others to help make things seem a little spooky!

A performance is a bit of an aerobics session for me as I am moving around a lot, acting things out, playing the instruments and getting the audience to join in with me. I often work up quite a sweat but for me there's nothing better than the feeling that the whole audience is on my side, children and adults all experiencing that shared enjoyment of poetry.

On a visit to Iceland I discovered how much more goes into the performance of a poem than just the words. I listened to poems read in a dozen different languages. As I could not understand the words, I paid attention to body language, actions, gestures, sound effects, rhythms and dance. All of these were brought into play to put across the poems.

Brian Moses

What the Poets Say

'I want the children (and the teachers, the dinner ladies, the caretaker and the person who's come to mend the photocopier) to be excited by the possibilities of words to make you laugh until you cry. . .'
Ian McMillan

'I cope with [performance] nerves by making sure that I know my work really well and putting it over with confidence and clarity and volume.'
Tony Mitton

'I don't really get nervous before I visit a school, because, long, long ago I used to be a teacher and I still enjoy talking to children. I only worry about a) getting lost, b) forgetting my sandwiches, and c) being asked to use something scary like an interactive white board!'
Clare Bevan

'I love visiting schools nationwide and giving performances of my Poetry Show. It is interactive and everyone has a good time joining in the hand actions and chanting the choruses. One school I visited had an adopted guide dog and it attended my performance. After two poems it lay down, fell asleep, and snored loudly!'
Wes Magee

'I love performing – the best shows are when I've made things up on the spot (improvisation) and when teachers also enjoy themselves. My best strategy is to be myself and to let the poems speak for themselves, but also to give it some welly – there's no point in being quiet and reserved when you have 200 young people sat in front of you.'
Andrew Fusek Peters

'Bringing poems to life is great fun and a wonderful creative challenge. A poem, you see, has two lives: one on the page and one in performance. I spend ages working out how to perform each new poem – how to express it – with actions, or music, and considering the pace, the dynamics, where to put pauses, where to climb on the furniture. . .'
James Carter

'I think poetry should be alive. You should be able to dance it.'
Benjamin Zephaniah

Who Are the Poets' Poets?

I began writing poetry when I was eighteen years old. I discovered a book of poetry by three poets from Liverpool – Adrian Henri, Roger McGough and Brian Patten. That book changed my life.

Roger McGough has always been a great inspiration to me. His poems are clever and witty, he is an expert at wordplay. When I started reading his poems I felt that they spoke directly to me, were about things that interested me and best of all, I could understand them. Over the years I've discovered many poets whose work I really admire.

The Irish poet W B Yeats and the American poet Robert Frost are particular favourites. When I was teaching I discovered Kit Wright and Gareth Owen, and a book called *Late Home* by Brian Lee. Brian's book is sadly long out of print, but the poems are carefully crafted and all about his childhood. I recognize so much of my boyhood in the lines that he wrote.

There are many more poets whose work I admire and I often pick up a book, read a poem and think, 'Now why didn't you think of that idea – it was right under your nose.'

| Roger McGough has inspired many poets.

The poets' poets, in no particular order

Lewis Carroll, Gareth Owen, Ted Hughes, Roger McGough, Brian Patten, Walter de la Mare, James Reeves, Charles Causley, Allan Ahlberg, Robert Burns, Robert Frost, Robert Louis Stevenson. . .

Why are so many poets called Robert?

What the Poets Say

'I'm inspired by music and songs. You'll find loads of Beatles-isms all through my stuff. The Beatles are why I write poems and play guitar.'
James Carter

'I like Robert Frost, particularly his poem "Stopping By Woods on a Snowy Evening" which has a marvellous rhyme scheme and creates a wonderful word picture of snow and winter.'
Wes Magee

The Beatles, seen here in the 1960s at the height of their popularity, wrote words for their songs that made a deep impression on many people.

'The first poets to inspire me were the "nonsense" ones: Edward Lear and Lewis Carroll. I was also inspired by the short collection by J R R Tolkein, *The Adventures of Tom Bombadil*. It has some of the best wordplay ever.'
Mike Jubb

'Of all the wonderful poets I read, my favourite is still Robert Burns. He is a Scottish poet whose poems I learned as a child, and when I hear them sung or read today they still make the hair on the back of my neck rise.'
John Rice

'My favourite poets are Charles Causley, because I love his strange and beautiful ballads, John Keats because I studied him at school and so many of his words still echo inside my mind, and Walter de la Mare because his poems tell spooky stories.'
Clare Bevan

Are You Rich?

I have been asked this question on many occasions, sometimes accompanied by, 'Do you live in a mansion?' and 'Do you drive a limousine?' My usual reply is to tell children not to run away with the idea that all children's writers earn as much as J K Rowling (or as one writer once said, 'we're not all J K Rowling in it!').

Michael Rosen often visits schools to answer questions about his poems and how he writes them.

An Icelandic writer, Þorarinn Eldjarn, once told me that in answer to this question he always tells children that he is very rich because, 'It's the only way I know to convince them to become writers.'

There are often questions about fame. Children like the idea that they are meeting someone famous and are disappointed if I tell them that I'm not. I usually say that I'm not famous like footballers or rock stars but that I am probably quite well known in schools, libraries and bookshops!

Another favourite question is 'How much do you earn?' My reply is always, 'I'm not telling you, but you don't need to worry about me, I do okay.'

'How old are you?' is another frequent question. Nobody seems to believe me when I tell them that I'm ninety-three!

Occasionally there are more perceptive questions like the one I had recently in Wales: 'Do you write any poems that are just for yourself and not for publication?' I thought for a minute and then had to admit that I do, but not very often. The last one I wrote was in the hospital ward where my mother was very ill.

It is great to get questions though, particularly if they are the sort of questions that ask about my poems or particular lines in my poems. That is very satisfying and tells me that the children have already looked at my work.

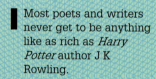

Most poets and writers never get to be anything like as rich as *Harry Potter* author J K Rowling.

What the Poets Say

'Not rich, not poor, not famous either and I haven't met J K Rowling!'
Paul Cookson

'Rich? Not in money, but maybe yes, in time. These days I'm mostly able to do the work I want to do, which in a way is the best kind of richness I can think of.'
Tony Mitton

'When school pupils and teachers see my display of books (in total I have written over ninety) they often ask, 'Are you a millionaire?' By way of an answer I take a few coins from my pocket and drop them on the table. 'My entire fortune and worldly wealth!' I tell them. The truth is, most books make but a small sum, that is, unless you are lucky enough to write a huge best-seller.'
Wes Magee

'Here are some answers to questions I'm often asked: no, I'm not rich; Liverpool Football Club; muesli; yes, my dog Judy really did write a poem – but sadly is no longer with us; yes, you can be *anything* you want to be when you grow up, but you have to realize that some things require a lot of work; I enjoyed being a teacher but I enjoy being a poet more; I wanted to be a rock star; I'm in a band and I play guitar and keyboards; yellow; the Beatles; my favourite day is Monday.'
Roger Stevens

'Not rich. But who cares? Even the cat doesn't mind as long as I earn enough to pay for her favourite food.'
Clare Bevan

'Not rich! Not even close! And I'm only famous in my own kitchen! If J K Rowling had written *Harry Potter* in rhyme, then maybe us poets would be selling more books now.'
Mike Jubb

Biographies (more secrets!)

BRIAN MOSES
(The author of this book)

I live in a tiny village in East Sussex with my wife and our daughters plus a loopy labrador called Honey, or Dustbin Dog, or Honey Houdini or the Honey Monster. She's a huge bundle of trouble and we all adore her!

I keep chickens at the bottom of my long garden and will readily talk chickens at great length to anyone who shows the slightest interest (and many people who don't!). I'm a bit of a chicken bore and know fascinating facts about chickens, like how to deal with invasions of red mite (it was like Glastonbury for red mites in my chicken house last year) and what to do if chickens get scaly foot.

I've supported Tottenham Hotspur since I was a child, through the bad times and the bad times, but I don't desert my team just because they feel at home in the lower reaches of the Premiership!

Latest book: *Walking With My Iguana,* an anthology of poems for performance, published as both a book and CD by Wayland.
e-mail: **redsea@freezone.co.uk**
websites: **www.poetryarchive.org** and **www.poetryzone.co.uk**

CLARE BEVAN

Clare Bevan used to have a friendly stick insect called Tutankhamun but now she has a grumpy speckled cat called Myfanwy (or Miff for short, which suits her as she's usually miffed about something). Clare lives in a cobwebby house in Crowthorne with her husband Martin and their son Ben.

Clare's favourite hobbies are, a) reading hundreds of books, b) riding round her village on a purple tricycle, c) walking for miles in search of the Amazing Ideas Shop, and d) dressing up in silly costumes and acting in plays. (In her last play she was a fierce queen, but she has also been a shy mole, Rupert Bear, a wicked witch, a magical sprite, and a noisy chicken.)

She also enjoys eating as many different flavours of ice cream as she can find. (Her best one recently was Green Marzipan!) Favourite Book: *More Fairy Poems* (Macmillan)

VALERIE BLOOM

Besides writing, Valerie loves reading (obviously), cooking (she makes a mean vegetarian curry and her Jamaican patties are not too bad either), gardening (but she'll never have enough time to do as much as she'd like). She wishes she could spend more time with her hundred or so bonsai plants and she enjoys playing word games (especially Scrabble and Upwords, but again she hasn't too much time for those).

JAMES CARTER

James Carter was born at an extremely young age. Finding himself on planet Earth he attempted to make sense of it all by reading comics and listening to the Beatles. At age fifteen he picked up the guitar and hasn't put it down yet. Ten years ago he began writing poems and hasn't stopped yet.

Alice is James' very strange but ever so loveable cat. Or, more likely, James is Alice's very strange but ever so loveable owner. When they first met in the pet shop, Alice the month-old-kitten jumped on to James' shoulder. She still does this. Trouble is, she's a lot heavier now and her claws are much, much more scratchy. Ouch. Of all the books James has ever done, his favourite is probably the CD version of *Time-Travelling Underpants* (Macmillan) as it's not only got poems aplenty but also some wild guitar music too. Find out more at **www.jamescarterpoet.co.uk**.

PAUL COOKSON

Paul Cookson has been the compere at several Slade fan-club conventions and their lead singer, Noddy Holder, has written an introduction to one of his books. He is official Poet in Residence at the National Football Museum and has poems published in the Everton match-day programme as well as being featured on *Match of the Day*.

Paul has two ukuleles and now writes ukulele poetry. His favourite book is *The Truth About Teachers* which he wrote with David Harmer, Brian Moses and Roger Stevens. 'I love the size of the book and the cartoons of David Perkins (he draws for *The Beano*, you know).'

JOHN FOSTER

John Foster's favourite things when he was young were a big teddy bear who was bald, because he cut off all its hair, and his cricket bat with which he imagined hitting sixes for England. He grew up in a village called Scotby, near Carlisle, and is a fervent supporter of Carlisle United. He is well known for his poetry performances as a dancing dinosaur and a rapping granny.

ANDREW FUSEK PETERS

Readers may be surprised to know that in his forties Andrew has taken up skateboarding again with a passion. He has also been included (finally) in the *Oxford Book of Children's Poetry* – and it's with a poem about when he did a great aerial in a California skatepark in the 1970s.

As a child he had a pet snake that kept escaping. The snake was finally found wrapped round a central heating pipe under his bed. 'After six months of no food he was alive but too weak to eat the live mouse we tried to give him. I wept and wept!'

Favourite book: *Mad, Bad and Dangerously Haddock* (Lion) – the best of Andrew's poetry, full of both silly and serious stuff. Find out more at **www.tallpoet.com**

Biographies (even more secrets!)

MIKE JUBB

Mike Jubb lives in Hampshire with his wife Sally and their cat Bagpuss! (Well, he says he didn't give him that name! Can you imagine how embarrassing it is when he has to go out in the garden calling Bagpuss! Bagpuss!?) Apart from nursery rhymes, the first poem Mike learned off by heart (at the age of eight) was 'Jabberwocky' by Lewis Carroll. He liked it because it has the Jubjub bird in it. It became his favourite poem and he can still say it off by heart. He's also written a poem in the same style called 'The Jubjub Bird's Lament'.

Favourite book: *The Ghost of My Pussycat's Bottom*, available from Amazon or from the publisher on **www.back-to-front.com**

JUDITH NICHOLLS

Judith Nicholls was born in an old white cottage opposite a farm in a tiny village in Lincolnshire. For many years, until recently, she lived in an old white cottage in a Wiltshire churchyard – but this one did have an inside loo and a bath!

When she first started school she hated it and used to yell at the gate to go home – but she remembers her first teacher, Mrs Mullins, and the way some of the cheekier children answered, 'Yes Mrs Mulliiiiiinnnnns' when she took the register!

WES MAGEE

Years ago, in a school where Wes worked, there was a boiler room in the cellar. The room was spooky, gloomy and dusty, and was rumoured to be home to the Boiler Room Beast. One boy said he saw it and drew a picture to prove it. His drawing was so good (and scary) that the head teacher had it framed and hung on the wall. The picture remains there to this very day. . .

TONY MITTON

Tony Mitton says that he is the age now when there's not much left for him to do except write. It's what he spends most of his time doing. When he's on holiday he goes walking with his wife, boots on, over the hills, plod, plod, plod, yap, yap, yap.

When he's not writing he's either redecorating the bathroom or doing the shopping and cooking the dinner. His wife hates shopping and cooking, but Tony finds they make quite a good break from writing. 'And I do like eating and drinking,' he says, 'so someone has to do it.'

Tony was once a primary school teacher, which used to be a nice job, till the government came along and spoiled it!

BRIAN PATTEN

Brian likes gardening and swimming in the sea. He loves snorkelling and wants to try aqua diving soon. He has been paragliding too.

He always wanted to be a writer, and he loves to travel. In the last few years he has crossed deserts, been in jungles and up the Andes. He has also followed Darwin's voyage to the Galapagos Islands.

JOHN RICE

John Rice is a Charlie Chaplin fanatic and likes to dress up as Charlie (with a very accurate costume!) now and again for parties and other events. 'The good thing about doing that,' John says, 'is that Charlie was a silent comedian in the old films so I don't need to talk to anyone. I just mime. Strangely enough they mime back (even though they are allowed to speak!).' Also, John's biggest secret is that he was once a spy!

John's favourite book is *Guzzling Jelly with Giant Gorbelly* (Macmillan). Find out about him at **www.poetjohnrice.com**

MICHAEL ROSEN

Michael was born in Pinner, Middlesex, the same day as the church next door to his family's house was burnt down, or so his mother told him. He began training to be a doctor but soon realized that it wasn't for him. After studying English at university he joined the BBC but that didn't work out either. His first book of poetry for children was called *Mind Your Own Business*. He liked that title because when people asked him what his book was called he could say, 'Mind your own business!'

Two strange facts about Michael that you may not know are that he can't live without green warty pickled gherkins, and that he can slide his top lip one way and his bottom lip the other. Michael was appointed Children's Laureate in 2007.
His website is **www.michaelrosen.co.uk**

ROGER STEVENS

Here are some more answers to questions that Roger is often asked about himself: I get my ideas from a poetry supermarket – you can find them in the chill section, next to the adjectives aisle; rhythm is more important than rhyme; yes I am very handsome – I don't know why, I was just born like it.

BENJAMIN ZEPHANIAH

Benjamin Zephaniah says that when he was a child and was caught reading a book in his house, his parents would come along and say, 'Haven't you anything to do?' These days he writes books himself and poetry is what he loves writing the most. When he performs his poems he recites from memory.

When asked what he was like at the age of 11, Benjamin says that he had an enquiring mind, that he was always asking questions (particularly ones that began with the word 'why') and that he was 'fascinated with girls'!

Glossary

Dictaphone: hand-held voice recorder used to dictate letters or record thoughts for future reference.

haiku: a Japanese type of poem that is three lines of words making just 17 syllables in all.

laureate: a person honoured with an award or prize. The word comes from the tradition of placing a wreath of laurel leaves on the head of a winner.

near rhyme: words that don't quite repeat the same sound but are near enough to suggest a rhyme. There are various sorts of near rhyme such as off rhyme, half rhyme and eye rhyme.

rhyme: different words which repeat the same sound, usually at the end of alternative lines of a poem.

rhyming dictionary: a dictionary that provides words that rhyme with the main words listed.

rhythm: a regular beat which can be made by the syllables of specially arranged words when spoken.

stagecraft: the skill or art of performing on stage.

thesaurus: a type of dictionary that provides words of similar meaning to the main words listed.

writers' block: a state in which a writer is unable to think of what to write.

Index (Entries in bold type refer to a photograph)